Creative

Conversation Starters
for **couples**

by Robert and Pamela Crosby

Honor Books
Tulsa, Oklahoma

Second printing, over 15,000 in print.

Creative Conversation Starters for Couples
ISBN 1-56292-587-3
Copyright © 2000 Robert C. Crosby
A Focus on the Family® book published by Honor Books
P.O. Box 55388
Tulsa, Oklahoma 74155

This book is dedicated to
Mr. and Mrs. Robert C. Crosby Jr. and
Rev. and Mrs. David H. Krist
For giving us homes full of love,
full of wonderful conversation,
full of life.

INTRODUCTION

While the two of you were dating, you probably talked all the time, leaving few subjects untouched. And it can still be that way!

This book has been designed to help you keep the conversation flowing and intimacy growing throughout your marriage. It contains insights that will inform and enrich your relationship and dozens of great questions to help you reveal your innermost hopes, dreams, interests, and fears.

You may wish to read this book together with your spouse or on your own. If you use at least one question each day at an appropriate moment, you will soon find yourselves formulating your own great questions and discovering new ways to love and appreciate each other.

The Crosbys

Creative

Conversation Starters

Question-asking can be downright life-changing, can't it? Jesus Christ knew that and, as a result, used questions with amazing frequency. He asked questions like: "Who do you say that I am?" (Matthew 16:15 NKJV)

Great questions to ask—

Do you think an objective observer could tell
we are a Christian couple?

⸭

What do you most need from me to encourage
your growth as a Christian?

⸭

What steps can you and I take to ensure that our
relationship continues to be close—
both emotionally and spiritually?

How important is question-asking to
developing and cultivating a good marriage?
Very. Dale Carnegie once put it this way:
"You'll gain more friends in three minutes by getting
interested in other people than you will in three
months of trying to get them interested in you."
In a similar vein, you'll cultivate more intimacy in
your marriage relationship in three minutes
of thoughtful and considerate question-asking
than you will in three months of trying
to impress your spouse.

Great questions to ask—

Who had the most positive influence
on you as a child?

What famous person would you
most like to meet?

What one day would you love
to live over again?

9

Men and women ask questions all the time—at work and at play. A junior executive taps a senior associate for advice that will help him succeed. A first-year auto-body repair apprentice asks a master of the trade what he does to achieve a smooth surface. What motivates them both is the anticipation of a better grade, a broader understanding, a promotion, a better reputation, or greater respect.

Great questions to ask—

What is your favorite time of day?

What's the best book you've ever read?

What was the brightest part
of your day today?

Creative

Conversation Starters

Men and women ask questions outside the business world as well—in the neighborhood, on the phone, and at church. Topics can range from corporate policy to domestic insights to how to encourage a child's learning. But how often do you ask questions of your spouse?

Great questions to ask—

What are your favorite kinds of flowers?

Which cologne/perfume do you
most like me to wear?

What is your favorite season of the year?

Questions are invitations.
They welcome people and invite people in.
They encourage individuals to confide in us,
to unload, to dream, to dare, and to share.
They break through the stony surfaces
that keep us from growing close.

Great questions to ask—

If you could store up only one hour's worth
of memory in your mind, which hour of our
marriage would you want to remember?

Which Bible character do you think
I am the most like?

If you could have the autograph of anyone
in the world, whom would you choose?

Many wives and husbands are starving for intimacy in their lives. Rod Cooper, a Promise Keepers leader, pronounces *intimacy* as "into-me-see!" That's good. It says much about what intimacy brings and calls for. It also describes exactly what effective questions should draw upon. Undoubtedly, the man who chooses to give his wife genuine intimacy gives her much more than a marriage license. He gives her himself— unmasked, uncovered, and unlimited.

couple

Great questions to ask—

Which songs were your favorites
growing up?

If we could have two days to spend alone together,
how would you like to spend them?

Which of your hobbies makes you feel
the most relaxed?

Conversation
Starters

Intimacy cannot be forced, driven,
or demanded. No remote control exists that,
upon command, can summon the thoughts,
concerns, feelings, and longings of a spouse's
soul. Intimacy is something that must be drawn
out in a relationship. Proverbs 20:5 says,
"The purposes of a man's heart are deep
waters, but a man of understanding
draws them out" (NIV).

Great questions to ask—

What is one thing you would like to try
that we've never done before?

❖

What is your idea of a nice quiet evening at home?

❖

What is your idea of a great night
out on the town?

What is intimacy?
Intimacy means that I know
who you are at the deepest level,
and I accept you.

Great questions to ask—

What in your life today brings you the greatest
sense of joy and fulfillment?

When do you feel the most loved?

What was your most difficult
experience as a child?

Intimacy is reaching out to
understand your spouse in the face
of busy schedules, different personalities,
embarrassing secrets, and past hurts.

Great questions to ask—

If you could possess any
extraordinary talent in one of the arts,
what would you choose?

❖

How would you describe your parents' marriage
while you were growing up?

❖

How did you get along with your parents
during your teen years?

Conversation Starters

Intimacy is a block of time
given freely or sacrificially to the one
to whom you have made vows.

Great questions to ask—

Do we plan enough "fun times" together to keep you motivated and encouraged?

What can we do to keep our marriage fulfilling and fun?

What is the most spontaneous, fun thing we have ever done?

Intimacy in marriage is
"an unhindered emotional closeness
in our inmost being through which
husband and wife are continually sensitive
and responsive to one another."

Gloria Okes Perkins
"Intimacy: A Realistic Approach"
Discipleship Journal

Great questions to ask—

Do you feel that I build you up with my words?

Do you feel that I treat you with
kindness and thoughtfulness?

In what ways do I show you how
much I truly appreciate you?

Intimacy is opening up to your mate
when he/she reaches out.

Great questions to ask—

Do you feel I'm willing to be
vulnerable with you?

❖

Which strengths in your life bring you
the greatest satisfaction?

❖

What is the best way for me to
encourage you every day?

Conversation Starters

Intimacy is being spiritually, intellectually, and emotionally familiar with the deepest nature of your partner's mind, soul, body, and spirit.

Great questions to ask—

How does it make you feel when we pray together?

What practical steps can we take as a couple
to be accountable to one another?

What is one thing you wish we had more
time for in our lives?

31

"Intimacy is the fusion of two distinct lives headed in two distinct directions into a single journey of one flesh."

Patrick M. Morley
Two-Part Harmony

Great questions to ask—

If we could just drop what we're doing and
go do something fun, what would it be?

When do you feel the closest to me?

What is the single most important thing
you need from me right now?

There is so much that we can ask
and need to be asked. Wise spouses take
determined steps to lay aside their own
concerns and consider the current
needs of the other.

couples

Great questions to ask—

What is your favorite chore
to do at home?

❖

In what ways can I make you feel
more confident as a parent?

❖

How can we slow down our busy lives?

Conversation
Starters

"You should never stop chasing the person you marry," says one pastor-friend, Ron Domina. As a matter of fact, the Bible says it this way: *"Therefore shall a man leave his father and his mother, and shall cleave unto his wife: and they shall be one flesh"* (Gen. 2:24, KJV). The Hebrew word for "cleave" is *dabaq,* which literally means to "follow close" or to "pursue hard."

Great questions to ask—

What is one of the most adventurous things
you've ever done?

If you could spend one whole day with anyone
in history, who would it be?

As we grow older, how can we keep the passion
in our relationship as strong as it is now?

Intimacy flourishes when a man and
a woman refuse to end the adventure of
asking great questions, listening closely,
and sharing deeply. The benefits of
doing so are not to be missed.

Great questions to ask—

If you could be president of the United States for one day, what's the first thing you would do?

✦

What was your first-grade teacher like?

✦

When do you feel the most cherished by me?

The husband who chooses to
treasure the soul of his spouse not only
strengthens his wife but also his marriage
and, ultimately, himself. By the same token,
when a wife respects her husband's
insights and opinions, it strengthens
his sense of significance.

Great questions to ask—

What role did prayer play in
your home as a child?

❖

Are there any treasured traditions you feel
we should be developing in our family?

❖

In your opinion, what makes a great parent?

Conversation Starters

Questions invite your spouse
to confide in you, to open his/her life
to you more fully. Perhaps, in a real
sense, the essence of marriage occurs
when a spouse compassionately,
carefully opens a mate's soul.

Great questions to ask—

In what ways has our marriage changed
you as a person?

What aspects of our life together were the most
challenging for you when we were first married?

When do you feel the most beautiful/handsome?

Questions lead to a more accurate view of the family's real needs. The mate who bravely chooses to tap into a spouse's soul will undoubtedly be confronted at times with hard truth. Ultimately, the only way a man or woman can accurately diagnose a family's needs is to take a close look at the untapped potential that exists within that family.

Great questions to ask—

Do you feel we spend enough time talking
and sharing our lives with each other?

❖

What can we do as a couple to change
the world in which we live?

❖

How can we be better stewards
of our money as a family?

Questions adjust your expectations
of your spouse. Unrealistic idealism works
against intimacy. On the other hand,
grace cultivates it. Perhaps one way to
define grace is "realistic acceptance."
Great questions help us discover what
is true about our spouses.

couple

Great questions to ask—

What do you think I expect from
you as a marriage partner?

Do you feel that I am a good listener?

What do you think I most need from you?

Conversation Starters

Questions open the door for your spouse to verbalize concerns, unload worries, and relieve stress. Wise and blessed is the spouse who provides a marriage partner with a safe place, a refuge, in which to express some of the struggles that build up each day.

Great questions to ask—

How full is your "emotional bank" today?

What impact is the pace of our lives currently
having on our marriage? . . . on our kids?

If you could change your life,
what would you change first?

Conversation Starters

Questions give a spouse an invitation to express honestly. The right question can validate a woman's strongly felt opinions and create an atmosphere in which she can safely express them. It can also give a man the accepting atmosphere he needs in order to express what's on his mind.

Great questions to ask—

When it comes to communication, in what
ways are men and women different?

❖

Do I most often approach marriage as
a "giver" or as a "taker"?

❖

Do you feel there are any unresolved
issues in our relationship?

51

Questions draw upon a spouse's dreams, longings, and desires, creating a clear agenda for ongoing encouragement. Many men wonder, *How can I encourage my wife? What can I do to lift her spirits?* Many wives wonder, *How can I build my husband's confidence? What kind of support does he most need from me?* The best answer we know is to *stop wondering* and *ask.*

Great questions to ask—

In what ways can I demonstrate
my respect for you?

How can I lift your spirits and make you laugh?

What questions do you wish
I would ask more often?

Conversation
Starters

Questions assist greatly in getting
to know the soul of the person you
married—the real person inside. If indeed
"they shall become one flesh," as the
Bible says (Genesis 2:24; Ephesians 5:31,
NKJV), it is God's intention that husbands
and wives initiate this process again
and again in deeper and more
meaningful ways.

couples

Great questions to ask—

How do I generally make you feel when we're
around other couples?

Are there any issues you feel we
really need to discuss?

How can I make you feel more secure in my love?

55

Questions do more than merely
draw upon opinions; they draw upon
God-given talents, spiritual gifts, and
abilities. The spouse in your life is not only
your spouse but an *individual* as well.
Celebrate your differences!

Great questions to ask—

When you think of the next ten years,
what are you most excited about?

What goals would you like us to accomplish
in our marriage in the next year?
. . . five years? . . . ten years?

What do you feel are your greatest
gifts, talents, and abilities?

Questions inspire more questions
and intimacy is a two-way street.
Don't attempt to ask your spouse great
questions unless you are willing to answer
a few yourself. The more you get to
know one another, the deeper the roots
of your marriage will grow.

Great questions to ask—

What are your three greatest strengths?

What do you feel are my three greatest strengths?

In your opinion, what are the five most important things a man needs to understand about a woman and her needs? . . . vice versa?

Creative

Conversation Starters

Ever had a conversation with your spouse that fell flat? When you ask vague, dull, unrefined, or off-the-top-of-your-head questions like "What do you want to do tonight?" or "What do you want for dinner?" the response will usually be just as dull. "Oh, I don't know. What do you want for dinner?"

Great questions to ask—

What was the most memorable date we ever had?

If you and I went on a date together with only ten dollars to spend, what would you like to do?

In what ways are you different from your parents and siblings?

Get beyond "yes" or "no" questions.
Ask for specifics. Great questions not only
search out facts; they also engage the
personality, mind, or opinions of another.

Great questions to ask—

What is your earliest memory?

❖

What is your most treasured memory
of childhood?

❖

What is the kindest thing anyone
ever did for you?

We tend to ask "why" questions much too early in a conversation. Like a submarine suddenly diving to the ocean floor without adjusting the cabin pressure, "why" questions can roll over barriers much too quickly. Let your spouse unwind after a tough day, and then start out with non-threatening questions. Your most important role when your spouse is stressed is to be a good listener.

Great questions to ask—

What was the best part of your day?

What was your greatest challenge today?

What can I do to help you right now?

Creative

Conversation Starters

Before asking your spouse a question, examine your motives. Consider the Scripture that says, *"A word aptly spoken is like apples of gold in settings of silver"* (Proverbs 25:11, NIV). The word *aptly* not only implies the right words and the right timing, but also the right tone. Your questions are important, but so is the place and manner in which you ask them.

Great questions to ask—

When it comes to the things that build a marriage, what are the best tools you and I have going for us?

How can we develop and strengthen a spirit of friendship in our marriage?

Do you feel we are standing as a united front before our children?

Test the water before diving off a
bridge. Respectfully and carefully consider
the levels of your spouse's openness
and vulnerability. The most effective
question-asking begins in the *shallow*
end of the pool (favorites, fun,
fond memories, family, friends), then
gradually goes deeper (feelings, finances,
failures, fears, the future, faith).

Great questions to ask—

What's your favorite musical group?

Do you feel that we spend enough time
doing things as a family?

What one possession do
you most cherish?

Great questions are invitations.
Take ample time to wholeheartedly
listen to your spouse's responses. People
can usually tell whether they are being
heard or merely humored.

Great questions to ask—

What values are we passing on
to our children?

How can we make our marriage
more of a true partnership?

Am I usually available and accessible when
you need to talk about something?

Conversation Starters

Often a day in the life of a
husband and wife can be poles apart
emotionally and experientially. The wise
man or woman takes time to consider
the feelings and experiences that may
have filled the other's day.

Great questions to ask—

How can I best reconnect with you and the kids
when I come home in the evening?

❖

What three things can I do to "build our home"?

❖

What tends to come first in our household?

As you head home at the end of the day,
consciously lay aside your workday and
fill your mind with thoughts of family.
Wonder about what each family member did
during the day and what they may need.
You and your family will be glad you did!

Great questions to ask—

What would you like to do tonight as a family?

What kinds of physical contact bring you the greatest fulfillment in our relationship?

What is the craziest thing you ever did on a whim?

The best time to ask a question is when
your spouse is ready to respond. It will take
a lifetime to perfect the art of discerning
when it is the right time to discuss
sensitive issues in your relationship.

couple

Great questions to ask—

How can we be more patient
with the kids?

What would happen if we turned off the television
for one day? . . . for a week? . . . for a month?

At what seasons in our marriage have you
felt the closest to me emotionally?

Conversation
Starters

Ask clarifying questions.
Sometimes the first query doesn't
get the job done. Learn to follow up and
make sure you understand what the
other person is trying to say.

Great questions to ask—

Are you saying you'd like to spend
more time with me?

Are you sensing that I am out of touch
with our son and his needs?

Are you feeling that we need to
get help setting up a budget?

Conversation Starters

Make use of the "pregnant pause."
After you've asked a question, don't
be afraid to wait for the answer.
Give the question a chance to sink in.
To hurriedly interject follow-up comments
short-circuits the genuine responses
your spouse was just getting ready to
express. Ask; then wait. You may be
surprised at what you'll discover.

Great questions to ask—

What can I do to help you more
around the house?

What time of day is best for us to talk?

Do you ever feel the need for time
alone to think and pray?

"Most marital difficulties center around one fact—men and women are TOTALLY different. The differences (emotional, mental, and physical) are so extreme that without a concentrated effort to understand them, it is nearly impossible to have a happy marriage."

Gary Smalley
If Only He Knew

Great questions to ask—

Which responsibilities in our home do
you feel the most confident about handling?

How can I get to know and understand your soul—
who you are at your deepest level?

What do you think God expects from you?

Conversation Starters

In an effort to overcome stresses
or to feel better when facing them,
women tend to *talk it out,* whereas
men seek time and space to *solve their
problems alone.* It takes some adapting
to communicate with someone of
the opposite sex, but it's worth it.

couples

Great questions to ask—

What does a woman need most from a husband?

What does a man need most from a wife?

Are there any activities in my life that you would like to participate in that you don't now?

"Men . . . become impatient when
women talk about problems in great detail.
A man mistakenly assumes that when a woman talks
in great detail that all the details are necessary for
him to find a solution to her problem.
He struggles to find their relevance and becomes
impatient . . . he doesn't realize that she is looking
not for a solution from him but for his caring
and understanding."

John Gray
*Men Are from Mars,
Women Are from Venus*

Great questions to ask—

With which of our friends do you feel
the most comfortable?

Which holiday do you enjoy the most?

When was the last time you and I
had a really good laugh?

Here are some general things a woman should remember when communicating with her spouse:

1. When a man becomes uncaring or distant toward a woman, it is usually because he's afraid of something.
2. Men are naturally motivated to achieve goals rather than absorb moments.
3. In general, men fear nothing more than failure.
4. Men are motivated by feeling significant.
5. Men want to manage their own problems (the "Mr. Fix-It!" syndrome).
6. Men always want to "get to the bottom line."
7. Men tend to "report" more than converse.

Great questions to ask—

How can we teach our kids to be
more effective listeners?

＊

How can I tell what mood you're in?

＊

When we have a discussion, what steps can we take
to make sure we stick to the issues?

Conversation
Starters

"What women don't know about [men] is that they need to have a reason to talk. They don't talk just for the sake of sharing. But when a woman talks for a while, a man will start to open up and share how he relates to what she has shared. . . ."

John Gray
*Men Are from Mars,
Women Are from Venus*

Great questions to ask—

Did you move often as a child?

❖

What do you remember about your
first day at school?

❖

How important were books in your household
as you were growing up?

Asking is not just an activity;
it is an attitude to develop. At its best,
asking is fueled by powerful motivators—
curiosity, wonder, interest, desire,
intrigue, and appreciation.

Great questions to ask—

If we looked at our marriage as a garden, what are some areas that need watering?

How can we keep our lives and our calendars synchronized?

What is your definition of forgiveness?

What keeps us from asking questions? Why is it that some spouses hesitate to ask and respond to questions? Why wouldn't they want to peer into the heart and soul of the person they promised to "love and to cherish . . . till death do us part"? Perhaps the answer is that asking great questions and communicating openly is something that must be learned.

couples

Great questions to ask—

If you could own the world's largest
collection of something, what would it be?

Did your family have pets when you were growing up?
What was your favorite?

Were you very athletic as a child?

Conversation Starters

One reason some people have problems communicating is that as children, they were reprimanded for talking. Compassion for your spouse can help overcome these developed inhibitions and open the floodgates to the soul.

Great questions to ask—

If you could personally witness any event in history,
which one would you choose?

❖

Do you remember any stories about your grandparents
when they were children or teenagers?

❖

How do you feel television affects our relationship?

97

Another factor that keeps many spouses from asking questions is the misconception, "If we love each other, we shouldn't have to ask." Nothing could be further from the truth. Great marriages necessitate great conversations. They find their genesis in strong and open communication between two people.

Great questions to ask—

In what ways have we become more alike
through the years?

In what ways have I changed since
we first got married?

How do you feel about the way we
resolve issues in our relationship?

99

According to the Bible, the best way to
receive is simply to ask. Whether praying
to God or cultivating a relationship
with your spouse, few things will open
doors and connect hearts like asking.

Great questions to ask—

Which one of our possessions
would you say you are most attached to?

❖

How much monthly income will we need
to live on when we retire?

❖

Have your greatest lessons in life been learned
"in the valleys" or "on the mountain tops"?

Creative

Conversation Starters

More often than not, life's opportunities come to those who ask. A lovely young lady's hand has gone to the suitor who proposed, rather than the one who hesitated or shied away. The thriving new business venture has been launched by the entrepreneur who raised the right questions and took the right steps.

Great questions to ask—

What are five essential values we want our kids
to embrace above all others?

How can we preserve, protect, and develop
our time spent together as a family?

How much work should our children
be doing around the house?

103

The most vibrant marriages are those which embrace the attitude of asking. These fortunate couples are eager to learn all they can about each other. In their minds, to live is to engage. The attitude of asking involves a passionate pursuit, an intriguing perspective, and wonderfully enriching intimacies. They are yours for the asking.

Great questions to ask—

Of all the gifts I've given you over the years,
which ones have meant the most?

What is the best novel you have ever read?

Would you prefer a picnic in the country
or dinner at a fine restaurant?

A lot *more* great questions . . .

Great questions to ask—

What is one thing I know how
to do that you would like me to teach you?

If you could be a contestant on any game show,
which one would you choose?

If you could be on the cover of any magazine,
which one would it be?

Conversation Starters

Great questions to ask—

Did you have an imaginary friend
when you were growing up?

What is your favorite sport?

Who were your heroes as a child?

couples

Great questions to ask—

What were your parents' favorite television shows
when you were a kid?

If you could recover any possession you've lost,
which one would it be?

If you could have witnessed any biblical event,
which one would you choose?

Great questions to ask—

What type of disciplinary style
did your parents use?

Do you feel that we discipline
our children effectively?

In what ways can we help our children
prepare for life on their own?

Great questions to ask—

In what ways are we teaching our kids to be good parents when they grow up?

✤

What steps could I take to make my relationship with your family stronger?

✤

What characteristics do you see in my parents that you hope I've inherited and will pass on to our children?

111

Great questions to ask—

In what ways are we teaching our kids good
manners?

What are your least favorite chores
around the house?

How do you feel about setting aside a weekly
family night—a night to update our kids, share
a devotional time, and pray as a family?

couples

Great questions to ask—

How well did your parents get
along with their parents?

In what ways do you think our parents' marriages
have affected our own?

Do you feel that I tend to show favoritism
toward any one of our kids?

Creative

Conversation Starters

Great questions to ask—

Do you feel we are doing enough to encourage our children's talents, gifts, and abilities?

※

What kind of person would you like to have as a son or daughter-in-law?

※

Do you feel that the kind of marriage we have affects the kind of parents we are?

couples

Great questions to ask—

How do you think our children would respond if
asked how they know their parents love them?

❖

What priorities tend to come first in our household?

❖

In what ways do you feel my actions and words
contribute to our children's self-esteem?

115

Great questions to ask—

Do you feel that we confront areas of concern in our children appropriately and adequately?

How do you feel the world's value system affects our kids' faith?

What things do you think the kids would really love to do with us?

Great questions to ask—

Do you feel we are training our kids to make proper choices and to be decisive?

What more can I do to make our children feel uniquely significant?

How does too much TV affect our kids' attitudes, values, and behavior?

Great questions to ask—

Do you have any ideas about how we can encourage creativity in our kids?

✤

Which do you feel is more important in our home—rules or relationships?

✤

When our children look back at our marriage one day, what do you hope they will emulate?

Great questions to ask—

How can we make our family
celebrations of Christmas and Easter more special?

How do you feel we can better prepare
our family for the future?

What are our children learning from our example
about generosity and sharing?

Creative

Conversation Starters

Great questions to ask—

How can we work together to build our children's confidence?

Do we feel that we bring out the best in one another and in our children?

What do you think about the friends our kids hang out with?

Great questions to ask—

How quick do you feel we are to
forgive one another?

How do you feel when you complete
a task successfully?

What friends of ours would you like
to have over more often?

Creative **for couples**

Conversation Starters

Great questions to ask—

Do my words and actions generally
build your sense of confidence?

⋄

How can you tell when people are really
listening to you?

⋄

What makes a marriage truly intimate?

Great questions to ask—

Do you feel we need to agree about everything to be really close?

❖

How would you feel about spending a weekend together by ourselves?

❖

Just how "together" do the two of us live our lives?

Great questions to ask—

What do you feel are the greatest differences
between men and women?

In what ways do you feel we are most alike?

Do you feel our differences complement
one another?

Great questions to ask—

What adjectives would you use
to describe our relationship?

❖

Is there any married couple on television that represents
what you wish our marriage was like?

❖

If you could choose, what would be the first thing
we said to each other in the morning and the last thing
we said to each other at night?

Creative

Conversation
Starters

Great questions to ask—

In your opinion, is our marriage closest to
a democracy (a sharing of power), an autocracy
(where one person rules), or a theocracy
(where God is first and foremost)?

❖

Do you feel our marriage proves the biblical
principle that "two are better than one"
(Ecclesiastes 4:9)?

❖

Would you like to spend time with some
of our friends this week?

Great questions to ask—

In what ways do you think we have
a great marriage?

How does it make you feel when I praise you
in front of others?

Are you satisfied with the way I communicate
my love for you?

Great questions to ask—

What same-sex friendship means
the most to you today?

❖

Would you like to sit down with me and look
through our wedding album together?

❖

Do you feel we could improve our
relationships with our neighbors?

Great questions to ask—

Does being around people drain you
or motivate you?

Which friendships have influenced
your life the most?

Who were your best friends
when you were growing up?

Great questions to ask—

Is there anyone you would like to
become better friends with?

⬩⬩⬩

What are the three most motivating things
anyone has ever said to you?

⬩⬩⬩

How do you feel I could improve
my listening skills?

Great questions to ask—

What comforts you when
you feel sad?

◈

What is the funniest thing you remember
about our wedding day?

◈

Who is the funniest person
you have ever known?

Creative

Conversation
Starters

Great questions to ask—

Are you content with our church life?

How would you like to grow spiritually?

Is there any subject you dread
talking to me about?

Great questions to ask—

Do you feel that I genuinely appreciate you?

Do you feel like we laugh enough at our house?

Is there any way in which I fail to honor you?

Great questions to ask—

What aspects of being married to me do you
find the most challenging? . . . the most exciting?

What do you find to be the most rewarding
aspect of parenthood?

When I say that I forgive you, are you sure
I truly mean it?

Great questions to ask—

On a scale from one to ten, how would you rate our marriage?

❖

Do you have any ideas about how we could make our marriage stronger?

❖

Which do you think is more important to me—your outward appearance or your inner qualities?

Great questions to ask—

What part of my personality or character
surprised you the most after we were married?

How can I best encourage your sense of
significance and identity as an individual?

When we're apart, how are you different from
the way you are when we're together?

couple

Great questions to ask—

What do you think about the
people you work with?

❖

In what ways does my frame of mind and disposition
affect the atmosphere of our home?

❖

What is your idea of a truly romantic moment?

Great questions to ask—

Do you think I am quicker to forgive
now than when we were first married?

Do you feel comfortable sharing your
deepest feelings with me?

What is my most irritating habit?

Great questions to ask—

What intrigues you most about me—my accomplishments and performances, or my personality and character?

⋄

What goals in life do you think motivate me the most?

⋄

What experiences do you and I share that tend to renew our closeness and sense of intimacy?

Great questions to ask—

Would you say I'm attentive to you
and your needs at home?

❖

Are you content with our way of life?

❖

If you could change one thing about
this country, what would it be?

Great questions to ask—

How well do you sleep at night?
Are you getting enough rest?

⁘

Do you ever feel that life is overwhelming you?

⁘

What do you enjoy most
about married life?

Great questions to ask—

Who do you feel closest to at work?

❖

What do you most want from our marriage?

❖

Do you feel that we complement
one another?

couples

Great questions to ask—

Do you feel that any of my activities
have too much importance in my life?

Do you feel comfortable with the way
we spend our money?

Which one of my friends do you like the best?

Creative

Conversation Starters

Great questions to ask—

What daily disciplines can I help you strengthen in your life? How?

❖

When do you most feel like a "conquering hero"?

❖

Do you feel I am a person who keeps my promises?

couples

Great questions to ask—

What is most important to your sense of security—
money or relationships?

❖

If you had to name the funniest purchase
you ever made, what would it be?

❖

If you had to name the wisest purchase
you ever made, what would it be?

Great questions to ask—

If you had to donate everything you own to a
charity, which one would you choose?

How well did your parents handle
their finances?

When is the best time for us to talk
about our finances?

Great questions to ask—

Do you have any concerns about
our retirement years?

❖

If our income increased by ten-thousand dollars next
year, what would we do with the extra money?

❖

In what ways do you feel we could ensure
that our children have a solid work ethic?

Great questions to ask—

Where would we cut our expenses if
our income suddenly decreased?

Do you feel that we pray together
as much as we need to?

What is your most urgent prayer
request right now?

couple

Great questions to ask—

How would you feel about
simplifying our lives?

Do you ever have trouble accepting a compliment?

How would you like our lives to be different?

Creative

Conversation Starters

Great questions to ask—

How do you relate differently
to your parents as an adult
than you did as a child?

How good are you at delegating?

What is your biggest pet peeve?

How good are you at delegating?

Great questions to ask—

What would you suggest to mellow
my temperament?

❖

What would you say is the best decision
we have ever made together?

❖

What one thing in life right now makes
you feel the most hopeful?

Great questions to ask—

Was there ever a great and inspiring teacher in your life?

Are there any secret dreams you have never shared with me?

How can I encourage your ability to dream, discover, and dare new things?

Great questions to ask—

Do you think I take myself too seriously
or not seriously enough?

Do you feel you can talk to me about everything?

What successes would you like
to repeat or exceed?

Great questions to ask—

How will our lives change after
the kids leave home?

What home improvements would
you like to see us make?

What is your greatest fear about
growing older?

Great questions to ask—

What do you think our children
will be like in twenty years?

If you ever had the chance to start a business
on your own, what would it be?

If we were planning a grand vacation,
where would you want to go?

Creative

Conversation Starters

Great questions to ask—

What do your feel is our family's
greatest strength?

What do you feel is our family's
greatest weakness?

What things do you feel you
do better than me?

156

Great questions to ask—

In what ways can we make a real
difference in our community?

❖

How can we use our resources to further
the cause of Christ?

❖

At the end of our lives, how do
we want to be remembered?

FOCUS ON THE FAMILY®

Welcome to the Family!

It began in 1977 with the vision of Dr. James Dobson, a licensed psychologist and author of best selling books on marriage, parenting, and family. Alarmed by the many pressures threatening the American family, he founded Focus on the Family, now an international organization dedicated to preserving family values through the life-changing message of Jesus Christ.

For more information about the ministry, or if we can be of help to your family, simply write to Focus on the Family, Colorado Springs, CO 80995 or call 1-800-A-FAMILY. Friends in Canada may write to Focus on the Family, P.O. Box 9800, Stn. Terminal, Vancouver, B.C. V6B 4G3 or call 1-800-661-9800. Visit our Web site at www.family.org.

We'd love to hear from you!

ABOUT THE AUTHORS

Married for more than seventeen years, Robert and Pamela Crosby are especially fond of asking questions of each other. The Crosbys are the parents of four children—Kristin,  Kara, Robbi, and Kandace. They reside in Burlington, Massachusetts, where Robert serves as the pastor of Christian Center Church.

Additional copies of this book and other titles by
Honor Books in partnership with Focus on the Family®
are available from your local bookstore.

Also available in this series:

Funtastic Conversation Starters for Parents and Kids

If you have enjoyed this book, or if it has
impacted your life, we would like to hear from you.
Please contact us at:

Honor Books
Department E
P.O. Box 55388
Tulsa, Oklahoma 74137
Or by e-mail at info@honorbooks.com